In Loving Memory Of

Forever in my heart!

Dedicated to beloved, sweet Remy, and to all the beautiful souls we are lucky enough to have as our four-legged family members

"What we have once loved we can never lose; they become a part of us."

Details About My Friend

Name:

Nickname:

Breed:

Color:

Favorite Treat:

Favorite Toys:

Best Personality Traits:

What I Will Miss The Most:

"You were my
favorite hello,
and my hardest
goodbye."

The story of how you came into my life is...

When you passed away
I felt...

Describe the burial arrangements

Tender thoughts
Sweet memories
My sweet
Forever Pet

My favorite memory with you is...

You made me smile when...

Lessons you taught me

"We're taught that
Angels
have wings,
but the lucky ones
find out they
actually have
Four Paws."

I will memorialize you by...

The happiest memory
I have of you

Build a list of songs
that lift your mood

I don't judge
I don't hate
I don't hold grudges

I DO love you
Unconditionally

I am your
Fur-Ever Friend

When things get tough,
I want to remember

My favorite story about you is...

I laughed the first time you...

The toughest part
of the day is

The best part
of the day is

Write about something that triggers sadness

Write about how to overcome your sadness

There's an empty
space where
you used to lay

And pain in my heart
that won't go away

I miss you my friend

I will pamper myself today with...

Write the words you need to hear when you are feeling sad

Write about things you wish someone would say to you

The nicest thing that someone said or did for me was...

Pick five words to describe how your heart feels

Celebrate successes in your journey through your grief

List your friends and family to share memories with

"The Best Therapy
Has Fur and
Four Legs"

Write about one thing you look forward to

My favorite quotes about pets

What did my favorite quote mean to me

Your unconditional love made me feel...

The greatest lesson I learned from you was

Write about something that
helps when things are hard

Since your death
our family doesn't...

One thing I loved doing
with you was...

When I'm alone, I ...

If I could change one
thing it would be...

If I could talk to you,
I would ask...

This grief has taught me...

The ways I have grown through this experience are...

A fun activity I will do for myself is...

My understanding of this experience is...

A favorite keepsake that reminds me of you is...

What advice would you give a friend who lost a pet

Describe how this loss
has made you feel

I struggle with...

The thing that helped the most through this experience was...

Write about a victory
you had this week

Make a list of all the things that lift your spirits

Write about something kind you can do for yourself

Favorite Pics Or Doodles

Favorite Pics Or Doodles

Favorite Pics Or Doodles

Favorite Pics Or Doodles

Favorite Pics Or Doodles

Favorite Pics Or Doodles

Favorite Pics Or Doodles

Favorite Pics Or Doodles

Favorite Pics Or Doodles

Favorite Pics Or Doodles

Favorite Pics Or Doodles

Favorite Pics Or Doodles

Favorite Pics Or Doodles

Favorite Pics Or Doodles

Made in the USA
Las Vegas, NV
25 November 2021